Handling Grief

A Christian's Ongoing Journey with Loss

THOMAS F. SLEETE

HANDLING GRIEF
A Christian's Ongoing Journey with Loss

Critical Mass Publishing
Fairfax, Virginia
www.criticalmasspublishing.com

Cover Photo: Channing M. Jones
Cover Design: Anabel Bouza
Layout: Rachel Greene

ISBN-13: 978-1-947153-04-2

This book is dedicated to my children, Tyson, Channing, and Shelby in addition to my granddaughter Ellie and any other grandchildren who might come along in the future. It is also dedicated to all those who, like me, have lost a spouse or loved one whose passing is overwhelming.

"One is the loneliest number that you'll ever do..."

THREE DOG NIGHT

Foreword

I met Tom and Moe Sleete when they visited a service at our church in Fairfax, Virginia several years ago. Then they came back.

Every Sunday.

Along the way, we became acquainted. We discovered common roots in Michigan, a love for the Detroit Tigers, Vernors "pop", and those unique Motown coney hot dogs (sometimes spelled "Koneys," no doubt to editor Sleete's chagrin). Tom's father was a pastor. So was mine. Preacher's kids from Michigan.

Then there was the "history" thing. I'm a history buff (some would say, Geek), so the fact that Tom was an accomplished history teacher—well, that ensured that we would become more than clergy and congregants. We became friends. Good friends. They became a fixture sitting near the front each Sunday. Tom helped edit some of my books.

Tom's what they call a "Master-Teacher." The best of the best. A teacher of teachers. Their time in Northern Virginia was always designed to be temporary, Michigan was calling them all of the time.

They eventually moved back—but kept in touch. And they never left our hearts.

When my grandmother died in Michigan in 2012, Moe drove about an hour from their home across town to spend time with my family at the funeral home. Unexpected, but so appreciated. And so very typical of Moe.

The night she passed from this life into the presence of her Lord and Savior in January 2017, Tom called me. He was brokenhearted. But it was clear to me that he did not "sorrow as those who have no hope."

Over time, he began to process his thoughts about Moe, life, death, and grief by writing. This book is the fruit of that effort.

And chapters are still being written in Tom's heart—as is the case with all of us who have suffered loss.

Rev. David R. Stokes
Fairfax, Virginia
March 2018

Acknowledgements

In this journey through loss and the composition of this book, many have helped in so many and varied ways. As I try to list these inspirers, I know that I will accidentally omit someone and for that, I apologize. Please know that these entries began as a blog on wordpress.com and, through more than one person's suggestion, they have evolved into this book.

First and foremost, I thank Jesus Christ, my Lord and Savior. Without Him, there is no way I that I would have made it even this far since Moe's passing.

My family, listed in the dedication, are the ones for whom I originally composed these entries, in order to show them how I have dealt with the loss of the woman we all loved so dearly. Their help in editing was invaluable.

My daughter-in-law, Anabel, whose artistic genius created the cover from a photo by my daughter Channing.

My friend, Pastor David Stokes, who provided me with the ability to get this project into print. Through criticalmasspublishing.com he has graciously and skillfully guided me in this process. The publishers are, without any doubt, the definition of "user-friendly" and wonderfully helpful. Not bad for a couple of Detroit preacher's kids.

I would be remiss if I did not mention my brother, Jeff Sleete, and my sister-in-law, Carole Descheemaker, who have been prayer warriors and sounding boards on the entire journey.

My deepest thanks to Dan Mountney (whose suggestion started the entire writing process), Joe Brandell, Pastor Phil and Amber Bassham, and the many others who have been incredibly supportive and gracious.

Finally, this is for you, Moe. My inspiration and muse. I love you Babe. Always have. Always will. See you soon.

"...for the greater the love the greater the grief, and the stronger the faith the more savagely will Satan storm its fortress."

DOUGLAS GRESHAM

Preface

On January 20, 2017, at 7:27pm, my wife Moe died. She was the love of my life and my best friend, lover, fan, encourager, wise adviser and so much more. One month after she went home to be with the Lord, I wrote the following:

For 38 years we shared everything; joys and triumphs, tears and losses, victories and defeats, tasks and arduous labor, friends and those who hurt us, all the vicissitudes of life.

I've lost my Dad and Mom, Clary and Joyce (my father-in-law and mother-in-law), Jan (Moe's sister), Tim (one of my best friends); so many I loved and who were so very dear to me, but nothing, NOTHING, compares with this. It is emotional, spiritual and, yes, physical in its sense of loss. It is being hit full speed by the emotional freight train.

But through it all there has been one constant. Through the chasms of grief and loss to the moments you think you might get through this, from the uncontrolled sob when she ought to be there to the peace of knowing she is no longer in pain, it is constant. The "still, small voice" of the Lord telling me that He is with me. That He shares all of this with me. That He will never let me go.

So many have said that I am an "honorable man." I know that I am only a sinner saved by Grace who has tried to be and do what his Savior commands. I fail miserably but His elegant sufficiency carries me on.

I loved so deeply, on so many levels, in so many ways, the woman He gave me. I had the joy of bringing her to Him and baptizing her. I know that I WILL see her again and we will spend thousands of years just...talking.

But, for now, the hole in me cannot be filled. The Holy Spirit has its place secured in me but the shattered shards of my broken heart hurt so.

Three things I always said to her...

I love you, Moe. I always have, I always will.

I'll lose everything, but I'll never let go of your hand.

Meus Bonus Amicus Deus Consultrix (My Good Friend God Provides)

> *I kept my promise, I walked her home.*

It is now over six months since the worst day of my life. People ask me how I'm doing. I resist telling them the whole truth (because who really wants to hear the agonizing details?) and I just say, "One day at a time."

Trite? Yes. True? Definitely. But along the way there have been lessons I've learned and so I've decided to put pen to paper and write about them.

"Only love keeps one from forgetting."

DIETRICH BONHOEFFER

Weeping Works, To a Degree

We men want to be seen as tough. Be leaders. Show strength.

And that is good.

But when a loss of your most profound love strikes, it is okay to let yourself go and cry. I remember crying at the funerals of loved ones. I also remember speaking at four of those funerals and realizing how hard it was to express what I truly felt and not weep in front of the gathered mourners. But as one of my pastors once taught, we have the perfect teacher in Jesus. At Lazarus' grave, Jesus wept.

And He knew that Lazarus was going to be back in five minutes!

C. S. Lewis wrote, "What sort of lover am I to think so much of my affliction and so much less about hers? Even the insane call, "Come back," is all for my own sake. I never raised the question whether such a return, if it were possible, would be good for her. I want her back as an ingredient in the restoration of *my* past. Could I have wished her anything worse? Having got once through death, to come back and then, at some later date, have her dying to do over again? They call Stephen the first martyr. Hadn't Lazarus the rawer deal?"

To have your eyes fill with tears when you hear "your song", or go to a place you both loved. Perhaps reaching for the phone to call her, or so powerfully miss her laughter at your shared humor. To ache in your loneliness and, well, you fill in the blanks, is okay. It is like a pressure valve that alleviates some of the stress and agony.

"Even in our sleep
pain which cannot forget
falls drop by drop upon the heart
until in our own despair
against our will
comes wisdom
through the awful grace of God."

AESCHYLUS, *AGAMEMNON*, AS PARAPHRASED
BY ROBERT F. KENNEDY

Beat Back Your Subconscious

For months, I wasn't sleeping well. I would awaken in the middle of the night, dreaming of and experiencing that hospital room at Moe's death. Try as I might, I could not stop the vivid dreams from recurring.

I wrote this in my journal: "Almost six months since Moe died and I am still fighting a battle. Why do I awaken so many mornings, early, and I'm right back in that hospital room, with her as she is dying. I know that I'll never forget it, but WHY do I have to keep reliving it in my mind?"

I hated it.

And then, one night, I got fully fed up. I had prayed for deliverance from the thoughts and an idea came to me. When I again awoke, I said out loud, "I've had enough", and I got up and went to my desk. After praying, I opened my journal and began writing out all of the wonderful events and feelings from our marriage. All that I treasured about her and us. How we laughed-oh how we laughed-and those beautiful times we had.

I wrote and I wrote.

After five and a half pages, I put down my pen, went back to bed, and slept through the night.

I haven't had the problem since.

So, in my experience, fond and loving memories kick the crap out of bad ones.

*"Wisdom is the reward you get for a
lifetime of listening when you would
rather have talked."*

MARK TWAIN

Just Listen.

I remember asking my Dad, a Baptist pastor, what I should say to a friend at his father's wake. My Dad said, "Don't say anything. Just be there and *listen*." The grieving will ask for advice, or help, if they want it or need it.

The Lord is opening doors of opportunity for me regarding this and I am determined to be there for those who are hurting.

By listening to my friend that day, I made an impact. He came to my Dad's wake, not long after, and asked me how I was able to cope with my loss. I told him that I knew that I'd see my Dad again because of the promises of Jesus Christ. Though not a complete unbeliever, my friend heard those words and a few years later I was thrilled to receive a letter from him telling me that not only had he become a Christian, but he was even teaching a Sunday School class and that my confidence in seeing my Dad again had been the ignition to his acceptance of Christ.

However, I must add sadly, the following. There are those with good intentions who should never speak to the grieving. When they approach and ask how you're doing, you can see in their eyes that they aren't truly listening, they're just preparing to unload their story onto you. I've been told about so many other deaths of friends, family, acquaintances, celebrities, _pets_, and people they've read about. I've been told about the illnesses they have, the medications they're on, the treatments their significant other is undergoing, their own dire situation, and so much other information non-essential for me. I've been told how GOOD I have it because their situation was SO MUCH WORSE than mine. Grief isn't a contest. It is NOT an Olympic event.

Sorry, folks, your therapy is not what the grieving need. They need a shoulder on which to cry, a hand to hold, and someone to listen.

Period.

Listen.

"Why didn't you come to me first?"

VITO CORLEONE, IN *THE GODFATHER*

Fruit Baskets.

They are wonderful, but there is a lesson to learn first.

Ask if the grieving have one before sending one. We got four lovely, delicious-looking ones. All at once.

We didn't have the time to open a fruit stand, so we had to take on the duty of trying to give so much of it away.

Ask.

"It is clear that the individual who persecutes a man, his brother, because he is not of the same opinion, is a monster."

VOLTAIRE

In My Case, Please Keep Your "Thoughts" to Yourself.

I received so many wonderful cards from family and friends. And meaningful gifts, too. The overwhelming majority of them told me that they were praying for me and my family. Those prayers are treasured and the pearls of great price that one can provide. If not in person, then at the Lord's throne, I will hug each and every one who prayed for us. With joyful abandon.

But there were a very few that bothered me, as a man well known for his faith in the Lord Jesus Christ. They were the ones who wrote, "Sending positive thoughts your way."

Really? Thoughts?

Okay, thanks, I guess. Appreciate the card.

I know I'm being too tough on people who don't share my faith. I know that they care and I know that is the way they express it. But they should know how empty those words are to one who believes.

So, I'll just thank them and pray for them.

"I am not so sure that I believe in the "power of prayer", but I do believe in the power of the Lord who answers prayer."

DONALD GREY BARNHOUSE

Have it out with Him. If you're angry, tell Him. If you're feeling lost, tell Him. Ask for help. Call on Him constantly and without ceasing. He's your FATHER!

While Moe was in the hospital, I shared Matthew 7:7 with her. "Ask and it will be given to you; Seek and you shall find; Knock and it will be opened to you."

Once, during her two weeks of hell in the Cardiac Intensive Care Unit, I brought Moe's Bible and it fell open to a couple of verses on which she had underlined and noted. My eyes are watering now as I write the verses next to which she had drawn stars:

1 Peter 5:7 "…casting all your anxiety upon Him because He cares for you."

1 Peter 5:10 "And after you have suffered for a little while, the God of all grace, who called you to eternal glory in Christ, will Himself perfect, conform, strengthen, and establish you."

Daily engagement with God's Word and in prayer are so necessary, valuable, and required. They maintain our connection with the Lord because without connection there can be no communication. So many times in my study, God's Word has met me right where I am.

On the 40th anniversary of our meeting, Friday May 13th, 1977, I needed alone time with God. So, I went to the quietest place I know. The graves of my Mom and Dad. If tranquility had a home base, it would be there.

I talked to God, prayed hard, and begged Him to show me what He wants me to do, where he wants me to go, and just what my life should become. I don't believe that I have to "reinvent" my life, I just have to live it for Him.

I sat and waited.

And, after a time, in my mind, I heard a voice. It was quick and its subject wasn't anything about which I was thinking.

I know it was God seeing my agony and honesty. He was clear in what He wanted. The voice said, "I want all of you."

I knew what He meant and what I had to do. Refocus on priorities, find a new church home, spend more time in prayer and His word, stop trying to eat myself to death, have more patience with others, be more focused on the eternal and not the temporal, help others, tithe more, get out, get active, and more.

And I've listened to that voice since I've become even more dedicated to being a Christian man, father, friend, and loved one, since I've embraced my grief and loss with the sure knowledge I've had all along, He has opened the floodgates of blessing on my life.

"It was too perfect to last, so I am tempted to say of our marriage. But it can be meant in two ways. It may be the grimly pessimistic-as if God no sooner saw two of His creatures happy than He stopped it. But it could also mean 'This had reached a proper perfection. This had become what it had to be. Therefore, it would not be prolonged.' As if God said, 'Good; you have mastered that exercise. I am very pleased with it. And now you are ready to go on to the next.'"

FROM *A GRIEF OBSERVED*, BY C. S. LEWIS

Read A Grief Observed, by C. S. Lewis.

Just do it. You'll know why when you do.

*"To each there comes in their lifetime
a special moment when they are
figuratively tapped on the shoulder and
offered the chance to do a very special
thing, unique to them and fitted to
their talents. What a tragedy if that
moment finds them unprepared or
unqualified for that which could have
been their finest hour."*

WINSTON S. CHURCHILL

Like the Boy Scouts, Be Prepared

Loss will continue to hit you. You won't see or feel it coming, it just will. I choose to embrace it at first, and then deal with it on different levels. Prayer works, so does remembering the positives, and knowing that Moe wants me to keep on going. I also remind myself that without great love, there cannot be great loss. I was blessed for so long, I do not get to complain. I just get to endure and carry on.

They say the Good Lord won't give me anything He knows I can't handle. Well, the Good Lord must think I'm a badass.

If you don't have these, get them now:

- A will
- A power of attorney
- A medical power of attorney
- A patient advocate form

We had them, and the hospital followed our wishes to a tee. No arguments. A family united.

Nobody guaranteed you tomorrow, or 15 minutes from now, either.

"The secret of life is honesty and fair dealing. If you can fake that, you've got it made."

GROUCHO MARX

Social Security Cheats

Six days after Moe died in January, Social Security went into our account and took back her January payment.

BUT, January's payment is for December. So, I had to go to their office and fill out a form to get it back-along with a whopping $255 funeral benefit. It took four months to get it back because, as the Social Security supervisor told me, "You are a low priority."

Interestingly, once I complained to my Congressman, I got reimbursed within six days.

I know that to the Lord a day is like a thousand years and a thousand years like a day. But to Social Security, six days is like four months.

"We are all faced with a series of great opportunities disguised as impossible situations."

CHARLES R. SWINDOLL

Lean on Loved Ones, They Love You Too

My three children were rocks during Moe's hospital time. They took care of everything for me so that I could totally focus on their Mom. They'd take turns sleeping at the hospital with me, they'd send me home to shower and nap, they'd prepare or get meals for me, and on and on. They were magnificent.

Once, when all three were at the foot of the bed, Moe said, "How blessed we are." And she was never more right.

I also spent time talking to Moe's sister. It helped so much to be able to weep, laugh, and share emotions with one who also shared the profound loss of the same person.

In addition to God and family, talk to someone else. Someone with wisdom and discernment and faith. Someone who will both listen and impart guidance.

You shouldn't do this alone, I don't care who you are.

"The two most important days in your life are the day you're born and the day you find out why."

MARK TWAIN

After a Time, Get Busy

If it is work, doing things around the house and yard, volunteering, or some other venture-get back at it. It will give you a focus, and most likely, the Lord will use it.

I was thinking about quitting being a consultant for the College Board after this summer. I figured I'd just see how it went. Well, it went alright. I have had my most successful summer teaching teachers, more than I've ever had. Such positive interactions and reviews, I can't believe it.

When He wants to guide you, He doesn't just crack the door open. He slams it open.

"The difference between one friend and no friend is infinity."

KEN BRUEN

Real Friends Cry

In grief, you find out who your friends really are. They weep over her passing, they call or write to find out how you are, they volunteer to do ANYTHING for you knowing that the offer sounds hollow since the one thing you want them to do is impossible, bring her back.

Real friends listen, care, act preemptively for your benefit, bring food, know what you need, don't ask just do, and love you in spite of the human wreckage you are at the time.

And, while I'm at it, CICU nurses are the most wonderful beings on this earth. They've entered a helping profession with caring hearts the size of which beggars the cosmos. Working 12 hour shifts and tending to all medical and comfort needs, along with monitoring progress or regress, they are exemplars of professional excellence, but with so much heart.

Immediately after Moe stopped breathing, and before my children got back to the hospital, I felt the hand of the hospital chaplain on my shoulder and he prayed with me. I also heard an almost silent sobbing. I thought it was one of my children, but it was the CICU nurse. Such compassion I have rarely seen outside a family.

I must also add one personal bit of information. Moe's heart never stopped beating until all three of my children got back to the hospital and into her room with her.

My wife. Caring mother to the very end.

Lord, I miss her so much. And my friends weep with me.

"Preach Christ. And if you must,
use words."

MARTIN LUTHER

I have determined to provide consistent evidence of the hope that resides within me with regard to my future with Moe and my life until then.

I do it by maintaining a positive attitude in my work as a consultant. If people didn't know that my wife had recently passed away, they would not know it by my attitude. I am positive, humorous, intellectually engaged, dedicated to rigorous instruction, and giving with my resources and time. In short, I try to be the teacher I always wanted to be (and have) for a class.

I do it by always mentioning how I could not continue in this process of loss without my faith. Most, in fact all of the over 100 teachers that I instructed this summer, were very positive in hearing how I cope. All but one, that is. He hated that I mentioned God in my presentations. Well, I hate to tell him, but when I die he won't be the one judging my life and I won't have to look in my Savior's eyes and answer for denying Him.

I do it by fulfilling the remaining promises I made to Moe. I know where I'm going to take her ashes this fall. I know that I will keep up on the house and sell it when it is time. I know that she was my one and only love and that there will never be another. Quite frankly, I am not interested in another who would just be a companion.

I do it by being ready with an answer, ready with a smile, ready to talk to others who suffer loss, ready to empathize with those who need it, ready to be a father and grandfather of whom both Moe and the Lord would be proud.

I do it because I must in order to be an example to my children, my grandchild, my neighbors, my friends, and those with whom I come in contact regularly. I want them to think that the faith I have is attractive and the confidence I have is catching.

"If earth is fit for laughter then surely heaven is filled with it. Heaven is the birthplace of laughter."

MARTIN LUTHER

I Know She's Laughing

How do I know that Moe is laughing? Pretty simple really. She is in a place, with the Lord, that is joy at its purest form.

Not only that, she loved to laugh here on earth. Together, we laughed about so many things. Goofy things our children did, malaprops said by friends or others, ridiculous situations in which we found ourselves, comedies on TV or in films and books, foibles of our own making, and so many other causes of laughter, they would be too numerous to name.

Another reason I know she's laughing is because I could always make her laugh. Many times inadvertently. I can just see her sitting around in Paradise along with my other loved ones and laughing at me right now.

At my feeble attempts at cooking which only has one rule, don't poison anyone.

At me for body surfing in La Jolla, California, two days last week. Oh, it was fun, but each morning as I awoke and my aching body screamed, "Hey, idiot, you may not feel 70 but your body is 70. So enjoy this for a while and get a grasp on reality." I know she's shaking her head and saying that I will never grow up.

At my disastrous ventures in gardening which she did so well. And I, to be honest, do not have any kind of plant or vegetation that I cannot eradicate.

At the stories that my guardian angel(s) tell her about me and how they've had to be inexhaustible in their efforts to just keep me alive this far.

At how I, so many times, attempt something around here and wonder aloud, "How did she do that?" My skill as a handyman is commensurate with my gardening acumen.

At how I frolic with our granddaughter, nonstop. Once my daughter told me that grandparents who babysit their grandchildren run less risk of getting Alzheimer's. I replied that that is because they die of exhaustion.

At the joy she shares with our loved ones that one day. To her soon we'll all be together and laugh as one, along with our Savior.

And because I know she is laughing, darn it, so can I.

"In a moment of decision, the best thing you can do is the right thing to do, the next best thing is the wrong thing, and the worst thing you can do is nothing."

THEODORE ROOSEVELT

Some Things You Can't Do Alone

Okay, I admit it. I can't do some things alone. The primary evidence against me is our house.

When Moe was alive, we divided up the work and upkeep on the house as equally as possible. Cleaning the floors, bathrooms, kitchen, carpets, furniture, oven and microwave, bedding, and so much more, repairs of all kinds, garden plantings and weeding, troubleshooting throughout the house, dishes, laundry, tidying, car maintenance, tree trimming, painting, trying to organize all of the "stuff" that belongs to my daughters, deck upkeep, keeping the house looking like something about which we could be proud, are just some of what keeping this house entails. And this does NOT include what we should do on a daily basis, except the dishes.

To be honest, she did more than her allotted half. To be brutally honest, there is no way in..........well, you know, that I can do this alone. Sure, I have help from my kids, but they have their lives and will soon all be gone from the house. And the fact that this is too much for one person to do is what awoke me at 1:30AM last night and kept me awake until 3:30AM.

I am NOT whining, I am just laying it all out there. If you think that life is going to just go on or continue as it previously had, you are dead wrong. Earthly responsibilities and necessary tasks will, at times overwhelm you.

Get help.

Demand help.

*"He sets on high those who are lowly,
and those who mourn are lifted to
safety."*

JOB 5:11

"Job looked down at me this year and said, 'Damn!'"

THOMAS F. SLEETE

2017 Stinks, Except for My Daughter's Wedding

When I look at the world this year, the following stand out:

- Hurricane Harvey and the horrific tragedy it has poured on Texas
- The lunatic in North Korea
- Gridlock and incompetence in Washington
- Charlottesville and Berkeley riots
- The further coarsening of relations between citizens in America
- Scandals in politics, sports, entertainment, social media, et al.
- The vanishing moral foundation of the nation
- And I could go on and on and on

And then, I look at what's hit me this year, so far:

- Moe's heart attack, two weeks of hell in the CICU, and death
- Moe's memorial celebration

- Taking her ashes to the place where we dreamed of living
- Food poisoning
- Three heart exams
- Jury duty
- Gigantic hospital bills, thank the Lord for health insurance
- Water heater dies
- Sump pump dies
- Both cars "needed work"
- I turn 70
- Bronchial infection
- "Significant narrowing" in an artery
- Bathtub leak into the basement
- Need for not one, but two, root canals
- Going through Moe's clothes
- A friend's suicide
- A cut that took forever to stop bleeding

This is only a partial list and doesn't even encompass some of the travails, illnesses, or problems that have struck ones I love.

So, yes, this year can be seen as awful.

But I must also acknowledge the blessings God has showered on me this year:

- The uncompromising love of my granddaughter
- The prayers of so many for me and my family

- The most successful summer of consulting for the College Board that I've ever had
- Connection with so many who have been supportive of my family and I
- The God-given ability to deal with the negative
- The joy and tears at my daughter's wedding
- Rest and relaxation on the Pacific Coast at the end of the summer
- The support and love of my children
- The opportunity to create this book. To hopefully be of assistance to others who grieve
- The fact that I'm pretty healthy for my age
- The fact that Moe and I were ready for this season with all the appropriate legal systems set up
- The overwhelming kindness of strangers who have helped me in situations like planning where I will spread Moe's ashes
- Wise counsel
- Deliverance from evil
- Prayers answered
- A relatively healthy heart
- And so much more

And there it is. Plain as day. God is in control. One of my favorite pastors is Charles R. Swindoll. He once wrote, "When you accept the fact that sometimes seasons are dry and times are hard and that God is in control of both, you will discover a sense of divine refuge, because hope then is in God and not in yourself."

Obviously, I can't say it any better. He is in control. He promised to never let me go. He never reneges on a promise.

I must be content.

But, honestly, I can't wait for this year to be over.

"When people talk, listen completely.
Most people never listen."

ERNEST HEMINGWAY

Practiced What I've Preached

Last night I went out for dinner with two men who have suffered recent loss. One lost his wife, a few months after Moe passed away, and the other has recently gone through a divorce. They are good friends and they both loved Moe.

I'm happy to say that, unless asked to contribute, I listened to and was there for them, especially the one enduring the death of his wife. We had a great time. We laughed at our memories of hilarious times, cried a bit, consoled, comforted, supported, and enjoyed each other's company while gaining strength from the bonding that took place.

I gained so much by just listening and I know that it was appreciated.

Mission accomplished.

*"Loss is made endurable by love and it
is love that will echo through eternity."*

JENNIFER WORTH

A Message

It happened out of nowhere. As I was taking down a shoe rack to give to one of my daughters, she discovered three boxes, one addressed to each of my children, and a couple of envelopes, one of which was addressed to me.

Moe composed these messages and thoughts back in either 2012 or early 2013. Each was personalized to its recipient. The boxes contained mementos, quotes, and love notes to the kids. Showing her wonderful sense of humor, she told each of them not to tell the other two, but that they were her favorite.

My envelope contained deeply personal messages and quotes for me, one of which is at the top of this entry.

As always, I will be transparently honest here and say that reading the messages was poignancy at its most extreme height and depth. Moe was so eloquent in her expression of her love for me.

Yes, I cried.

In a way, I felt like Michael Corleone in *The Godfather, Part 3*. "Just when I thought I was out...they pull me back in!" I was operating under the delusion that I was getting somewhat "used" to life without her. That my emotions were not as raw as they had been. That I had survived all the waves of grief.

Nope.

In addition to all the wonderful, loving, gracious words Moe wrote, as always, she threw me a lifeline. Her heartfelt touch gave me peace. In one of the notes she left, which Moe addressed to me in case I survived her in this life. I will close with the last lines of what she wrote:

"I so look forward to recognizing the light of your soul in the heavenly place we've been promised. Our Lord has blessed us so."

Me too, Babe. Me, too.

"Laughter and tears are both responses to frustration and exhaustion. I myself prefer to laugh..."

KURT VONNEGUT

Frustration

Frustration is a word with which I have become intimately acclimated. This comes from the fact that Moe is not there for me to talk to. I can't have the kind of deeply intimate conversation in which we used to be able to engage.

I know, I know, take my own advice and talk to God. Well, I do. Constantly. And He provides for me, far more than I deserve. But what I need is the kind of human conversation that provides immediate vibrant attention. That dispenses sage advice covered in wisdom and discernment. That is always in confidence and will never be revealed to another.

Conversation with Moe is not possible. There are those who say they talk to those who have passed. Using Scripture, I see that that is more an act of talking at a loved one, than talking to them because, again according to Scripture, those who've passed can't respond.

I have been overwhelmingly blessed with magnificent people in my life who are more than willing to listen to anything I want to say. My brother, my sister-in-law, my children, pastors, dear friends, all are there for me. But what I want, I need, to talk about are things that are so achingly personal and intimate to me that, to be frank, transcend boundaries I will never cross with another other than the one who was half of me.

I'm frustrated and I have only the following to say to anyone going through it, so far as my experience has been to this point. Toughen up. Bear down. And get used to burying those thoughts and feelings that you can no longer express. Dig them up and deal with them on your own, when you are able.

And, above all, laugh at them. It'll really tick them off.

*"I'll lose everything, but I'll never let
go of your hand"*

TOM WAITS

Touch

Moe came to me in a dream last night. She was standing by the bed, looking at me. Her black hair, just shoulder length and streaked with grey, was vibrant and full. Even her bangs. She wore her wire rimmed glasses, a black turtleneck with a dress jacket of an auburn hue, her silver crosses around her neck along with a decorative necklace. Oh it was her all right.

She was urgently pointing for me to go in some direction. It almost seemed nonsensical.

In spite of what she was indicating I tried to reach for her but, of course, she wasn't really there. And as I did, a powerful sense of loss hit me. I knew what it was that was gone, it was touch.

I deeply miss her touch. Our touching.

When we would hold hands wherever we walked.

How we would give each other three short and gentle squeezes on the arm for which each squeeze stood for one of the words, "I love you".

As she would massage my neck whenever we were in the midst of a long drive somewhere.

The way we would always gently awaken the other with gentle caresses of our hands rather than shakes.

As she would always touch me when she wanted to make a point in a discussion.

Her gentle caresses.

I miss those and so many more.

All I can say is that those are sensations that are forever gone. I will add this to Moe: Whenever you want to come back in a dream, please feel free to do so.

You know me, you'll need to write out where it is you want me to go in order for me to get it.

"When someone you love dies, and you're not expecting it, you don't lose her all at once; you lose her in pieces over a long time — the way the mail stops coming, and her scent fades from the pillows and even from the clothes in her closet and drawers. Gradually, you accumulate the parts of her that are gone. Just when the day comes — when there's a particular missing part that overwhelms you with the feeling that she's gone, forever — there comes another day, and another specifically missing part."

JOHN IRVING, A PRAYER FOR OWEN MEANY

Identify Your Losses

I'm reading a very helpful book titled, *Through a Season of Grief*, compiled by Bill Dunn and Kathy Leonard. In it they write, "You will miss so many qualities and facets of the person you lost that each will become an opportunity for grief." They go on to encourage readers to compile a list of those qualities and facets and say them aloud to God because only He can provide.

I think that this is a very healthy thing to do. So, here's only the beginning of my list of Moe's qualities:

- Biggest fan
- Lover
- Interior designer of our home
- Cook
- Companion
- Encourager
- Discerner of others' motives
- Wise counsel
- One who gets my awful jokes
- One who shares our private jokes
- One who truly knows me

- Source of comfort
- Friend
- Co-conspirator
- Repairwoman
- Guide through parenting
- Christian heart
- Desire for Godly understanding
- The little gestures
- Always there for me
- Appreciation of what I try to do
- Empathy
- Sympathy
- Heart for others
- Sharer of so many memories
- Our shared laughter
- aith and adherence to the Word
- Worship together
- Creativity
- Devotion to our family
- Humility
- Strength of character
- Forgiveness
- Tolerance of my foibles
- Hairdresser of what I have left
- Choosing clothes for me to buy
- Inner and outer beauty
- Communication with just a look
- Our oneness

That's just the beginning of my list. And it is a list I encourage all who grieve to compile. It is therapeutic.

I will close with something I wrote in my journal months ago. "You are and were my gift from God and the greatest blessing of my life. You were wise in all the ways I am foolish, seeing all I did not see, with a love both fierce and gentle, ever nourishing, all-encompassing but never cloying, my love eternal. I can't believe you chose to share your life with me. It is all or nothing without you."

"Every time you are able to find some humor in a difficult situation, you win."

AUTHOR UNKNOWN

Laughter, Again

I've experienced laughter at some of the most inappropriate times in my life. One was at my grandmother's funeral in the hills of Kentucky. Let me tell you that my grandmother was not, there's only one way to say this-an object of the love of her grandchildren. She was a tough woman who was not affectionate. I'll leave it at that.

My several male cousins and I are genuinely hilarious, especially when we get together. At the wake for my grandmother, we were all asked to leave the room because we were telling really funny stories about each other. Well, on the day of the funeral, we had to carry my pretty large grandmother to her final resting place on a snowy side of a hill in the cemetery. We'd all been laughing together in the cars on the way there but we were holding it together during the pall bearing. That is until my one cousin slipped and started rolling down the hill. I was shaking with glee when one of my female cousins, thinking I was weeping, gently touched my arm and told me "She's in a better place".

I lost it.

I tell you this because one of the lessons that Moe taught me was to be able to laugh at the worst of times. A few times during her misery in the hospital, she or I would say something that would crack each other up. When she was in pain on the first day in the hospital, they gave her Xanax. As she was finally being wheeled to a room, she said, "Tom, I'll say this for Xanax. It doesn't stop the pain, but with it you don't give a S_ _T." The orderly and I laughed out loud.

When she was in some of her worst pain, I went to war with one of the on-call doctors. I, in no uncertain terms, informed him that she had to get something more for pain and get it immediately. I actually feel sorry for the young physician, but this was my wife and I was not going to be denied. He prescribed Fentanyl, the drug that killed Prince. As the nurse's aide was injecting the drug, Moe said to her, "Wait, Fentanyl? What if I want to start singing *Purple Rain*?" Again, I started laughing out loud.

The night Moe died, we had to sit with the grief counselor and fill in the appropriate paperwork. It was a devastatingly heart wrenching time. Once it all was filled in by the counselor, my son read it over and discovered an error. She had listed me as the deceased and had my body consigned to the funeral home. I know that Moe approved as we all laughed at what could have been a really interesting process about to commence.

To the best of my ability, in order to honor Moe, I am going to try to live the code that was stated by that brilliant philosopher, Groucho Marx, when he said, "I, not events, have the power to make me happy or unhappy today. I can choose which it shall be.

Yesterday is dead, tomorrow hasn't arrived yet. I have just one day, today, and I'm going to be happy in it."

"The will of God will never take us where the grace of God cannot sustain us"

BILLY GRAHAM

Prayer Request

If you read this entry, I am requesting prayer. For emotional strength and the peace that only the Lord can bring.

In ten days, I leave for Montana to put Moe's ashes in the Boulder River, outside of Big Timber, Montana.

The Lord has made straight my path to honor Moe this way by sending my dear friend Joe Brandell, Ellen Brandell (Joe's daughter and a Montana expert), Brad Ehrman from Bozeman Fly who suggested the river, and Adam Wagner from Sweetcast Angler in Big Timber who is going to direct me to access points that will be beautiful and private. That will suit my needs.

The Lord's blessings on this coming journey have been so much more than I deserve. I know He is doing it for Moe. The prayers of my loved ones and their support have been invaluable.

Moe always said that she wished life were accompanied by a musical score. So, I'm going to bring my iPod and as I put my one true love's ashes in the river, I'm going to listen to a song we recently heard and loved. We both said it spoke to what each of us felt. And we each played it over and over.

The title of the song is "*How Long Will I Love You*". We heard in in the movie "*About Time*". The song was written by Mike Scott.

In this beautiful song, the question asked in the title is answered by saying that as long as the stars are above you, as long as the seasons follow their plan, as long as the sea washes up on the sand (and other eloquently stated parameters). It concludes that we will "relish this remarkable ride."

As for us, we relished it and I still do.

It's a great song and I highly recommend your listening to the movie version.

I will never stop loving you, Moe. And now the stars will be above you forever.

"I can do all things through Christ who strengthens me"

APOSTLE PAUL IN PHILIPPIANS 4:13

An Answer

I was listening to a sermon and this verse was used. It got me to thinking about what I've endured and what I will endure.

Paul was beaten, tortured, imprisoned, stoned, shipwrecked, scorned and ridiculed and eventually executed.

Kind of like what's happened to me, emotionally, this year.

There is also a perspective that must be gained here. Regardless of how bad I think I have it, there are so many more who are in far worse situations and conditions than I. The world of hurt does NOT revolve just around me. I am merely a pilgrim on this voyage not of my choosing, and I need to see all of my surroundings and vistas, not just what is right in front of me. 20-10 vision.

Besides, who am I to doubt Scripture?

"It's not about how hard you hit, it's about how hard you get hit and keep moving forward."

ROCKY BALBOA

"He replied, 'Because you have so little faith. Truly I tell you, if you have faith as small as a mustard seed, you can say to this mountain, 'Move from here to there,' and it will move. Nothing will be impossible for you.'"

MATTHEW 17:20

Lessons from the Journey

I am overwhelmed by the grace of God. He gave me the ability to not only go to Montana, but to be able to afford to go. Not stopping there, He provided wisdom and guidance from four people, three of whom were strangers, in getting to one of the most beautiful and apropos places on earth wherein I could place Moe's ashes. He provided so many wonderful Christian friends who prayed for me and my journey. When it was all completed, He provided me with wisdom about the journey gained from conversations with others.

As I look back at it, the trip seems like one big analogy. It begins with the fact that the location is known as a sacred place by American Indians. I wanted to tell them that it was infinitely more sacred now that Moe's remains are there.

The first day I was in Montana, there was a sleet storm on the route to Big Timber. How is that for ironic? Sleet. That aside, it made my going to Big Timber impossible.

The second day there was a snow storm that made the roads too dicey for a trip to higher elevation. I was beginning to worry.

The following day was gloriously beautiful. When I got to Natural Bridge, about 25 miles south of Big Timber, I was alone in all of this bounteous pulchritude. The only sound was the rapids of the Boulder River and the not distant waterfall. The peace I felt was so God-given and all encompassing. The wonder of His creation and His blessing on what I was about to do.

The trail from the bridge led downstream and up in elevation. This was not what I wanted. I wanted to be right at the water. After some searching, I noticed a lightly trodden trail through the grasses headed down river. After a short walk, I saw a barely discernable path that led down toward the river. I took it.

Once at the edge of the steep slope to the river, I halted. It was going to be a bit arduous, but it was what I wanted to do to honor Moe. Showing my love and ever present humor with Moe, I changed the words to Meat Loaf's song and, as I started my climb down, I sang "I would do anything for love, and I **WILL** do that."

A third of the way down, I had to leave my duffle bag for more maneuverability and to free a hand. Another third of the way, I set down the bag in which I was carrying Moe's ashes, keeping just the urn in hand, and said, "Okay, it's just you and me now, Babe." Immediately, I knew that I was wrong. The Lord was holding my hand and guiding my steps. And I thanked Him. It was a steep descent during which I grasped tree roots, bush branches, and even rocks, to steady myself in order to get to the water. Did I mention the muddy soil?

Once at the stunningly beautiful river, I paused. I prayed. I told Moe what I always said to her, "I love you Moe, always have, always will." And I let the ashes begin to drift away in the water. I listened to "How Long Will I Love You" (a song I mentioned previously) and also "Never Let Go", a song by Tom Waits.

In my mind, I could hear Moe say that it was such a beautiful place, but she would add, "Tom, you should see where I am now."

The tears filled my eyes, and my heart.

I climbed back up the river bank.

So what are the analogies?

First, God provides just what we need to accomplish His will. The people, the prayers, the financial ability, the support, all came from Him. Also, the path less traveled that He showed me when I had the faith to try another way.

Second, the fact that what we want to do is not always on His schedule. The sleet and snow delayed what I was in such a rush to do. Instead, He provided a day of incomparable beauty if I would just wait.

Third, a bit of wisdom from my friend Joe Brandell. As I went down the slope, I rid myself of baggage that I had been carrying. In accomplishing what I had promised, I was also ridding myself of my self-imposed anxiety and impatience in doing what I desired. Baggage I no longer needed.

Fourth came from my brother. In Rocky 6, "Rocky Balboa", the hero, talks to Paulie, his brother-in-law. In talking about the loss of his wife, Adrian, he says that there are still "beasts in the basement" of his soul with which he was dealing. Jeff, my brother, told me he hoped that by doing what I'd done, I have banished some of the beasts with which I've been dealing. As Rocky said at films end, "The beast is gone. The beast is out."

When one has an upcoming event which they have never encountered before, there is always a pressure one feels, even if they have positive anticipation of it. When I finally got to the top of the bank and looked back to the river, I felt a slight physical pressure lifted off my shoulders. I had done what I so wanted to do.

If you were one of those who prayed for me, I will never be able to thank you sufficiently. Just know this, He answered your prayer and He did so while showing the magnificence of His love for me, for Moe, and for you.

And now, I keep moving forward with the Lord guiding me.

*"There's a bit of magic in everything,
and some loss to even things out."*

LOU REED

That Hole in My Pierced Heart

Nobody ever told me that grieving was physical. They never let on that some of the loss that you feel has a corporeal component. C. S. Lewis wrote, "No one ever told me that grief felt so like fear. I am not afraid, but the sensation is like being afraid."

Just about every day, I think of something about Moe. It could be visualizing how she'd react to a situation or what she'd say about something I've done. It might be my wishing she were here to tell me how she did something, or just my making the bed and her side is undisturbed. Regardless, I could list so many other instances of how it occurs. That isn't the point I'm trying to make here.

What strikes me is that, at those moments, I feel the loss tangibly. Right in the heart. I think the best way to describe it is that I feel an emptiness. Almost the proverbial skipped beat of the heart. Not all-encompassing, just a passing sense of the irreplaceable.

I read a quote recently that helped me understand. The person said that you never get over the grief of losing a loved one, you just have to adjust to it. Adjust, yes. Fully content? Nope, ain't going to happen.

Blaise Pascal wrote *"What else does this craving, and this helplessness, proclaim but that there was once in a man a true happiness. Of which all that now remains is the empty print and trace?*

This he tries in vain to fill with everything around him, seeking in things that are not there the help he cannot find in those that are, though none can help, since this infinite abyss can be filled only with an infinite and immutable object; in other words by God himself".

This is the famous quote about the "God shaped vacuum" in each person's heart. Well, as I hope is obvious by now, the Holy Spirit has an established residence in my heart and soul. My vacuum is filled with my Creator, His Spirit, and His Son.

That, though, doesn't take away from the fact that I still feel-and I mean that in the truest, deepest, most intensely poignant sense of the word-a hollowness in my heart. It comes from the loss of the most wonderful gift, short of salvation, that He gave to this unworthy man.

The late Frank Deford, one of my favorite authors, expressed it best. Frank lost his wonderful little daughter, Alex, to cystic fibrosis. Decades later, he encountered a man who suffered the same loss. After sharing empathetic commiseration, Frank wrote the following: "About the loss of one's child, no, you never get over it."

Amen, Frank. It applies to all who were truly loved. I'll learn how to deal with this ache, but I know that it won't leave me until that glorious day when I get to hold her again.

"Anxiety does not empty tomorrow of its sorrows, but only empties today of its strength."

CHARLES SPURGEON

Here They Come

Today is November 1st and I am about to embark on my journey through what I'm told, and have experienced with the loss of others, is the most difficult time of year for those who grieve. Thanksgiving and Christmas without Moe. As a special bonus, they are followed quickly by the anniversary of her passing on January 20th. I can hardly wait.

1 Peter 5:7 is the anchor for me. "Cast all your cares on him, for He cares for you." Well, Lord, get ready for a seriously heavy load coming from me.

It is not a denial of faith to have moments of sadness at these times. It does not demonstrate a weakness of character to ache for the presence of your loved one. But, it must not and cannot be all consuming. I owe that refusal to so many. To my family who share my grief, to those to whom I witness the hope that lives within me provided by Christ, to my friends who pray and care for me in my mourning, and to the Lord who accompanies, encourages, and supports me on the journey.

Does all of that make it any easier? Emphatically, NO! But it does force me to take one step at a time and not be all-consumed by what is impending.

Will I be sad at times? Of course. But here I must make my stand.

Instead, I will savor the joys that are coming. To be with all of my family on Thanksgiving. To celebrate Christmas with my loved ones and all that Christmas means and provides. Even on January 20th, I must, and I will, celebrate the fact that my Moe entered into the presence of our Lord with great joy and rejoicing in Paradise one year prior. That does not demonstrate that I love Moe any less, quite the opposite. It shows that the faith I profess, and that I "preached" to Moe through all of our years together is of substance and built upon rock. I owe it to her as well as to the Lord.

I know that at times they will be bittersweet, but I don't need to fall into overwhelming despair. There is victory to be had.

*"There is more to this life
than this life."*

PASTOR CHRIS HODGES

I Fell

Yesterday and the day before, I fell. Not physically, but emotionally and spiritually. I became overwhelmed with all that I am facing and am in need of doing. All of the responsibilities, endeavors, work, family issues, loneliness even in and among those who love me, life choices to be made, all overwhelmed me. I was drowning and there was no lifeboat, just a hurricane tossed ocean as far as I could see.

I NEED to talk to Moe.

I NEED her wisdom, discernment, and advice.

I NEED her to be with me and help me as I endure, solve, or mess up all that is weighing on me.

I NEED for God to say, "Oops, mistakes were made. It wasn't her time. Death messed up, so just go to the front door and she'll be there."

But I CAN'T have that. And that hurts.

I hate death. I hate what it does to us, the living. I hate what it does to those we love who are taken by it. I hate the separation it enforces.

I hate the way it keeps creeping into my thoughts and memories. I hate its earthly finality.

Then, through simple words said to me by my sister-in-law, and preached to me by Pastor Chris, Christ obliterated it. I was renewed by the knowledge that this isn't all there is. There is a far better future for me. There is joy and glory in it. I'm simply marching forward until I get to spit in death's eye and tell him that he just doesn't matter. I have something far better on the other side of him.

It doesn't make this life any easier, but it does make it somewhat more endurable. C. S. Lewis once said that the most spoken phrase in Heaven will be "Aha!" We will finally get it. We will understand it all. And as I stand before the Jesus Christ, I want Him to look at me seeing what I've overcome and endured, how I've tried to be an imitation of Him in the lives of others, how I've been faithful to and witnessed for Him, how I've tried to use the gifts that He gave to me, and have him say, "Well done."

And then let me punch death right in the face.

"But we do not want you to be uninformed, brethren, about those who are asleep, that you may not grieve, as do the rest who have no hope."

I THESSALONIANS 4:13

"I can see for miles, and miles, and miles, and miles, and miles"

THE WHO

He Strikes Again

The Lord really knows how to lift you up. In the last couple of days He has reached out to my heart and given me, at the very least, some solace for the coming weeks.

The first was in a breakfast conversation with, as usual, my great friend Joe Brandell. Joe and I don't share the same styles of Christianity, he is a Roman Catholic and I am a born again Baptist, but we communicate on many levels of faith and are in agreement on voluminous issues. Just his being there for me and his willingness to both listen and impart discernment, are to be valued in their ability to help me keep my focus upward.

And speaking of upward focus, I strongly recommend listening to absolutely anything that evangelist/apologist Ravi Zacharias publishes. I listen to his podcast and am provided with spiritual ammunition that gives me hope and confidence.

Communication with my brother and the pastors in my life has jelped me put on the whole armor of God. Their prayers, concern, and confidence are treasured. In return, they entrust me with their prayer needs and a focus on others.

To be somewhat brief, I just want to add this thought. All of the aforementioned, along with staying in the Word, have helped to sustain me. They've enabled me to see so much further than this mortal imprisonment in which I am ensnared. I feel like Paul when the earthquake broke his chains and freed him in prison. He knew that he had more to do right where he was and he did not flee. Instead, he remained and witnessed to his jailer. Read it in Acts 16, from verse 26 on.

The Lord has spoken to me in so many ways, as I've written before. Truly paying attention to what His will is for my life, has given me a focus. No, I really can't get fully out of the imprisonment of loss, but I can see where this is all going. I must follow the path He has set to provide me with purpose and at least part ways with this soul crushing heartbreak of loss.

"Heroism is endurance for
one moment more"

GEORGE F. KENNAN

One Down, Two to Go

Thanksgiving is done and I didn't experience what everyone said I would during this holiday. In some ways it was so much worse and in others, so much better.

My lowest point came the day before Thanksgiving. It wasn't because of the holiday, but it was an accumulation of all the pressures and pain that I'd kept inside of me. The horribly vivid dreams of those last days in the CICU have come back with a vengeance, every night.

The emotional walls crumbled down inside me and I needed to go somewhere and scream.

So I did. I went somewhere private and let loose.

I had it out with myself, my pain, my worries, the pressures that are on me, Satan, and anyone and anything else that has contributed to my pain, stress, and agony. I had my brother and Moe's sister praying for me. It was something I needed to do in private and I could not, would not, let my kids in on it.

When I got home, I decided to rest in my room and read Scripture. The day before, I had left off after reading Philippians 2. When I got to two verses in Philippians, I simply stopped. I could not believe how appropriate they were for my situation. How they provided peace and assurance. Let me be clear here, I do not believe in coincidences. Here are the two verses that the Lord spoke to me through His Word.

Philippians 4: 7 *"And the peace of God, which surpasses all comprehension, shall guard your hearts and your minds in Christ Jesus."*

Philippians 4: 13 *"I can do all things through Him who strengthens me."*

What a truly amazing Lord I serve.

Thanksgiving Day was a joy with all three of my children, my son-in-law, and my granddaughter all here to enjoy such a wonderful feast that my daughters prepared. It was a day filled with laughter and joy.

When I said grace over the meal, I thanked the Lord for all of His blessings, too many to list here. I finished by thanking Him for the woman who brought all of us together.

Next up, Christmas. Followed by the anniversary of the worst two weeks and single day of my life. Yes, I miss her and the pain is so great, but it is endurable.

"Darkness comes. In the middle of it the future looks blank. The temptation to quit is huge. Don't. You are in good company...You will argue with yourself that there is no way forward. But, with God nothing is impossible. He has more ropes and ladders and tunnels out of pits than you can conceive. Wait. Pray without ceasing. Hope."

JOHN PIPER

A Ray of Light

Scripture tells us we can't communicate with those who have passed, nor they with us. But, I do believe they can petition the Lord to send us a feeling or thought that would be of help to us.

I had one last night.

I've mentioned that the vivid dreams, putting me back in that CICU room for the two weeks and Moe's death, have returned. Not as severely as before, but just a time I really do not wish to ever go through again. Nightmare is not a sufficient word for the reality that is forced upon my mind.

Then, yesterday night, I finally had a positive remembrance from that time that has been so uplifting for both my mind and my soul. Since this is my book, and my experience, I'm going to tell you about it.

After Moe had a major surgical procedure, her heart stopped that evening. It took electrical shocks to bring her back and, as is the requirement, she was intubated.

Moe and I always had an agreement. No longer than 48 hours on a respirator. Period.

When the 48 hours had come, I informed the doctor that I wanted the tubes removed. Right away. He asked me to wait another 72 hours. He was not ready for the question that I then asked. I said, "And what guarantees can you make for me if I let you do that?" He said that he couldn't and I told him that I gave my wife my word and that that takes precedence over his request. So take them out.

They gathered the required staff, and began taking the tubes out. The process is quick and, of course, Moe reflexively gagged as they did so. What I was not prepared for was how they then sharply, and loudly, badgered her with the order to "Say your name!" I now know that they do this to assure that the vocal cords suffered no damage in the procedure.

"Say your name!" She looked at them, somewhat sternly I might add.

"Say your name!" She turned to look at me, as I was bent close to her.

"Can you say your name?!" They were insistent.

With the most beatific smile on her face, and such great emotion in her eyes looking only at me, Moe reached out her left hand and gently touched my cheek, and said in a clear voice to me and me alone, "I love you."

Tears of joy filled my eyes. Glad that she could speak but so much more for the fact that she knew that I had kept my promise to her and that reinforced for her-I think-that I was going to be there for everything and that I would do what she wished, and nothing and no one would stop me.

Last night, I saw that look of love again and it so touched my heart and soul. I know that you asked for me to be reminded of it, Moe. Your love for me shines through this earthly fog and helps to give me hope and direction.

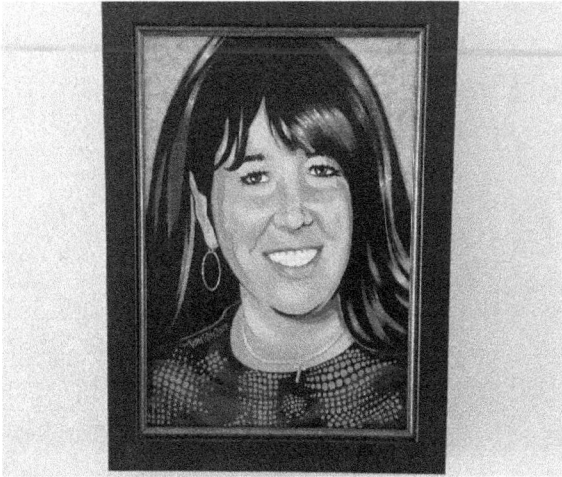

Moe: a painting by Tom Roy

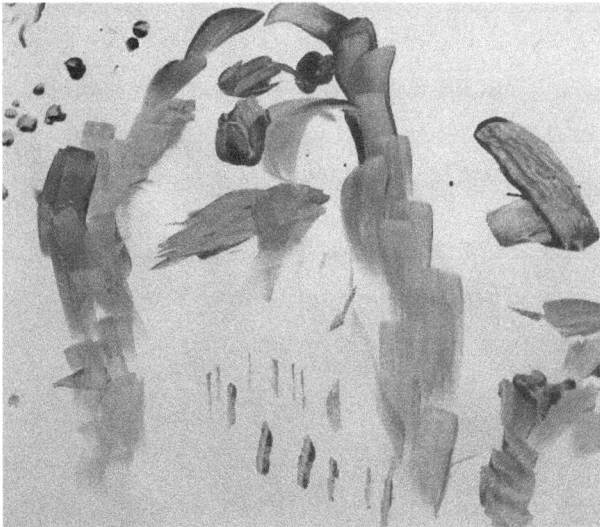

Gramma Moe: a painting by Ellie at age 3

The Reason

It's been ten months since Moe went home to be with the Lord. The same amount of time that I've been writing in my journal about my life since she's been gone. I started this book because a dear friend told me I should write about my experience.

So, today, I'm going to elaborate my reasons for creating the book.

The first, and must be foremost, is to bring glory to my Lord and Savior Jesus Christ. Without Him I would not have been able to get this far. His presence, His healing, His love, His compassion, His guidance, and His provision have been my foundation.

Next, I've written it because it has been therapeutic for me. It has given me a place to vent, express, commiserate, and try to provide a clear vision of how grief has affected me.

The third reason is my hope that this book can or will be a source of comfort, help, or inspiration in some small way for any and all who love me and Moe or, most especially, those who are also grieving. Grief is unique to everyone, but it might be a help for others to let them know that they are not alone in this emotional tumult.

Last, I do it to bring honor to Moe. The love of my life. The woman was and is so much to me. The one whose hand I will never let go of in my heart.

"No man has a good enough memory to be a successful liar"

ABRAHAM LINCOLN

I Lied to Her

It's confession time.

I lied to Moe.

And I did it on our wedding day, in 1978.

For some reason the following came to mind today, and it actually brought a smile to my face and awakening to my soul.

So, here are excerpts from the vows that are similar to the ones that were used with us. They're the classic and I'll add my annotation after each.

"To have and to hold from this day forward" (Yep, we did)

"For better" (Of course)

"For worse (Did that, too)

"For richer" (Teachers, we didn't get to do that)

"For poorer" (Got that covered, in abundance)

"In sickness and in health" (Obviously)

"To love and to cherish from this day forward" (Without any doubt)

"Till death do us part"

And that last promise is where I lied because there is no way on earth that I will let death stop me from loving and cherishing her.

Not going to happen.

Ever.

"The two most powerful warriors are patience and time"

LEO TOLSTOY

Where Has It Gone?

Billy Graham was once asked, by a college student, "What has been the biggest surprise of your life?" Almost without thinking he replied, "The brevity of life."

He wrote, "It's true, life is short, and the older you get the more you realize it. Events that happened thirty years ago seem like they took place yesterday-but when your mind turns to the future, you realize just how short life is."

I've been struck by this conundrum for the past week, on a lot of levels. First, and probably foremost, has been the fact that it has been almost a year since Moe died. Yes, it has been inconceivably hard, and yes at times it seemed to be an agonizingly slow process, but the eleven months have vanished like a vapor.

Another has dealt with my memories of our years together. Looking at pictures, going to places we'd been together, reading things we shared, seeing all the things she created and her personal touches on our house and the man I am, the list can go on. Add to that simply thinking of her and how she'd react to situations, missing her. Time seems overflowing with events and emotions but so incredibly transient.

I've been getting wonderful communications from former students in the recent weeks. Some knew of Moe's passing and some did not. Regardless, their gracious words about how I seemed to have touched their lives have been a godsend. And they also have struck me with the fact that these are mature adults who have taken a moment to reach out. Adults. How did that happen? For Pete's sake, I have former students who are 63 years old! Where did the time go?

When some people find out that I am 70 years old, and it's happened a lot in the last year, they say, "You sure don't look like you're 70." I don't answer with the typical "70 is the new 60" garbage, I simply say, "Thank you, but you should see it from inside here" as I point to my heart. I go away thinking that in my younger years I could not fathom being 70.

Songwriter Chris Cornell wrote the following lyric in his song, *Before We Disappear:* "Time ain't nothing if it ain't fast. Taking everything that you ever had." Right on both counts.

A major lesson on time has been in my reading. I've been deeply touched by a book titled *We Shall See GOD: Charles Spurgeon's Classic Devotional Thoughts on Heaven*, with commentary by Pastor Randy Alcorn. I know that I've already recommended *A Grief Observed* by C. S. Lewis and I stand by that recommendation. I would earnestly add this book to the list. I've been struck by his scriptural descriptions of what we will experience the two most important to me, at this juncture, are joy and eternity.

Joy and eternity.

God created us in His image. *His* image. And we have the ability to feel joy, smile, and most significant to me, laugh. There will be laughter in Heaven. He promised that He will wipe away our tears and they will be no more. That being the case, joy will reign supreme.

And then eternity. I will be with my loved ones for **eternity**. No time limit. No final buzzer. No finish line. Just all of us, with our Lord, doing what He desires with the talents He has given us, resting and ENJOYING all that He has prepared for us.

Forget the Hollywood crap about Heaven. Don't listen to the idiocy of projections that we'll be playing harps on clouds and being bored. Know that He said that we can't even conceive of what He has in store for us.

With that sure knowledge, I can more ably forge through this time of loss. This week it has personified the joy. I look forward to happening and sharing this joy with her.

Forever.

*"The song is ended but the melody
lingers on..."*

IRVING BERLIN

A Hat? Really?

My snow blower got a leak in the fuel line/carburetor and I had to take it to the repair shop yesterday. I won't get it back for four days. Then, of course, it snowed 3 to 4 inches last night.

So, back to the old fashioned way. I got my winter stocking hat, winter work gloves and a scarf, and it happened. Moe's hat and gloves were right below mine and I accidentally picked them up at the same time.

My mind flew to so many past winters. When I would be ready to go out and move the snow, she'd insist that I wear a hat and scarf along with a heavy jacket, boots, etc. As I'd be plowing, I'd always see her come outside all bundled up, grab a shovel-no matter the wind or weather-and shovel snow in areas hard to get to with the machine. Always wearing that hat, and those gloves.

And it hurt. A hat and gloves drove another of those arrows into my heart making me realize, for the umpteenth time, what I've lost and who and what I miss all of the time. I know that I've already written about how those realizations and feelings are physical as well as emotional. I fully understand that they are perfectly natural and go with the territory, because I so love her. But all of that doesn't make it pleasant or any easier.

Each season, holiday, event, crisis, task, sickness, happiness, special meal, and so forth bring along with them a small sense of loss in this first year of grieving. I get that.

I thought, "But, a hat? A hat?! Really? Is there nothing that she hasn't touched in my life that can provide some seclusion from these feelings?" It was then that I realized what I was truly saying. I was selfishly complaining about the fact that I had a wonderful partner who cared about me, worked with me, helped me, loved me, and with whom I got to share so many years. All of these things are part of what we had and who she was. How can I possibly object? I can't and I shouldn't. So, I won't.

Oh, yeah, One more thing. It's going to snow another three inches tomorrow, and I'll be doing this all over again, sans snow blower.

*"The true soldier fights not because he
hates what is in front of him, but
because he loves what is behind him"*

G. K. CHESTERTON

I Have You Covered

In the sixth chapter of Ephesians, Paul describes the full armor of God. It is the means by which Christians are to defend themselves from the evil of Satan and gird themselves for combat with sin and spiritual forces. It is interesting that in all of this armor, helmet, breastplate, sword, belt, foot covering, and shield, there is nothing covering the back.

There is an obvious reason for that. Our backs are to be covered by our fellow soldiers in this battle. They are there to provide a defense for us. How do they do this? With prayer.

I must confess that I have been a bit self-consumed during this past year. I have reaped such a bountiful harvest of prayer support from friends, family, and even people I don't know. All along the way I have been supported and held aloft by these warriors. I believe that I have been remiss in my duty to provide cover for others.

If you are reading this, you more than likely have suffered some form of loss that has touched you deeply. Your hurt is akin to mine. On my part, sympathy is insufficient. Empathy is inadequate. And my support for you has been deficient.

For that reason, I want you to know that from now on, I will lift you up in my prayers. I will ask the Lord for you to feel His presence, His love, His wisdom and His discernment, His plan for you. And, most significantly, His sharing of your loss.

We can't do this alone. We need all of the aid and comfort we can get. It starts right here.

Know that I'm praying for you and, as they say in the American military, "I have your 6."

*"I thought I could describe a state;
make a map of sorrow. Sorrow,
however, turns out to be not a state but
a process."*

C. S. LEWIS

No GPS

Elisabeth Kubler-Ross and David Kessler claimed that the five stages of grief are denial, anger, bargaining, depression, and acceptance.

Mary Todd Lincoln spent the last years of her life, one of them institutionalized, in "widow's weeds" (dressed all in black), in perpetual mourning for her lost husband and three sons. She used, or abused, medicines and spiritualists.

Comedian Patton Oswalt lost his wife, a woman he truly loved, and got engaged barely a year later.

In the Victorian era there were set rituals, including the wearing of black. The period for these was two years in the case of a lost spouse.

The Muslim period of mourning is 40 days as it is also in the Eastern Orthodox religion.

We Baptists, along other Protestant Christians and Roman Catholics, have no specified period of mourning.

In short, there is no GPS or roadmap for how long grieving lasts and with what it can be dealt. No universal step by step procedure. No "one size fits all". We each have to deal with it in our own way.

As for me, I will always have a portion of grief in my heart. That is, I must add adamantly, NOT a denial of the promise my Lord has made about eternity, it is only an expression of what I feel and what I experience, what I endure, and what I observe each day.

The days, now, are better than those surrounding our initial loss. But when "experts' try to tell me how long I will be bereaved, what stages I will go through, and when I can and should end my sorrow, I object. We all do it differently. All we can do for those who are in the midst of it is to be there for them, pray for them, and set an example for the hope that resides in our souls.

I didn't go through the steps of Kubler-Ross and Kessler. I wouldn't go to the extremes of Mrs. Lincoln or Patton Oswalt. I won't have a dress code or time clock from tradition. I'm just going to take this one step at a time and cling to my Savior's hand as I walk through the valley.

"I have finally found a place to live, in the presence of the Lord"

ERIC CLAPTON

M u s i c

I've mentioned before that Moe loved music. Whenever she worked around the house in the last few years, I could always count on her having her headphones in her ears listening to her beloved songs. I once came into the house without her knowing and, surprised, she told me that my timing was perfect since she was listening to *How Long Will I Love you.*

Today, I was listening to my iPod and I purposely steered away from songs that would sadden me. It's strange how certain songs just strike a chord (no pun intended) in my soul and encourage me in this time.

The first is *Amazing Grace*, the version performed by *Il Divo*, in concert. The words of the last verse gave me such peace and also showed me how much time I'll have with Moe.

"When we've been there ten thousand years

Bright shining as the sun

We've no less days to sing God's praise

Than when we'd first begun"

The other has been one of my all-time favorite songs. The title is *History Maker* by the group named *Delirious?*. It has been my inner theme song ever since I first heard it and also when I got to see them perform it.

"I'm gonna be

A history maker in this land

I'm gonna be

A speaker of truth to all mankind"

This song struck me because of my reaction to what someone said about this book. They said that it is extremely raw and I should perhaps limit my audience to just family and close friends.

I considered that option and rejected it.

One day, I will face the Lord. One of the things that He will ask is how I used any and all opportunities I had to take a stand for Him.

If ever I have been given that chance, it has been in the last year. Losing my love and having to stand alone in so many ways has shown me how much I need and use His support.

So, if you're going through it, too, consider it at the very least as an opportunity to show how much He means to you in this emotional devastation.

*"I am what I am and that's
all that I am"*

POPEYE THE SAILOR

My Speech

You don't really know me like Moe did, and in order to make the point I want to emphasize here, you really need to get to know who I am.

I'm 70 years old. Not decrepit, but certainly one with endurance.

I've taught over 6,000 students about American History in a career spanning 44 years in both middle and high schools. Students of practically every race, creed, color and religion, or lack of same.

I have instructed over a thousand teachers in how to teach Advanced Placement American History, in at least 15 states all across America.

I was a college student from 1965 to 1969 and that fact alone should be sufficient information for you to draw your own conclusions.

I've been an island of political conservatism in an ocean of liberalism in my profession.

I've experienced the unimaginable exhilaration of being at the birth of my three children along with the extraordinary joy of watching them grow from such wonderful little ones into admirable adults with strong character.

In this life I have spoken at the funerals of loved ones whose leaving greatly pained me; those who I long to see, to touch, to hear.

I've stood up to bullies, I've fought, and I've turned the other cheek.

I have read so many books, and continue to do so, that one could populate a good sized library with just those tomes.

I've experienced true friendship. Not the Facebook-social media-superficial type, but the call them at three in the morning and know that they will be there kind.

Over time I have had heroes, seen villains, and felt that ignorance is invincible.

I've travelled all over this country on a Harley-Davidson motorcycle, by train and airplane, and by cars ranging from a VW bus to a Camaro, all the while being stunned by America's natural splendor and the ever present decency of its people.

I have preached that talent is a gift, but character is a choice.

I've lived my life guided by the philosophy expressed by Hunter S. Thompson who wrote, "*Life should not be a journey to the grave with the intention of arriving safely in a pretty and well preserved body, but rather to skid in broadside in a cloud of smoke, thoroughly used up, totally worn out, and loudly proclaiming, 'Wow! What a ride!'*"

I've found that one truth in this life has never changed. It is so simple, yet it is so profound. It has guided me in my life's adventure, and will continue to do so until I take my last breath. It is something that I do not just believe. It is something that I know. And that wisdom comes from a little children's song which begins, "Jesus loves me, this I know. For the Bible tells me so."

So, why tell you all of this? Well, consider it a portion of "My Speech". In the wonderful film *Second Hand Lions*, the character named Hub, played by Robert Duvall, gives his young great-nephew his "speech". He talks about the things that a man must believe in, because they are the things that are worth believing in. That people are basically good; that honor, courage, and virtue mean everything; that power and money mean nothing; that good triumphs over evil.

Hub then holds back the lingering pain of having lost his wife so many years before, with so much emotion, and says the following: *"...and I want you to remember this, that love...true love never dies."*

So, yes, Jesus loves me. And one of the ways that He has shown it to me is by giving me a true love that will never die.

With that conviction, I will carry on.

"There are things known and there are things unknown, and in between are the doors of perception."

ALDOUS HUXLEY

A Christmas Thought

Three days until Christmas and for the first time in decades, I have stumbled upon a fresh revelation about this holiday. I know that everyone says that it will be the hardest one to get through, and I have to disagree. Our upcoming 40th wedding anniversary on July 8th, January 20th (the date of her death), her birthday, the anniversary of our meeting, and just about any day that brings a fresh reminder of my loss is just as poignant.

But yesterday, I had a thought that I would never have had if Moe weren't with the Lord. As I was thinking about Christmas without her, I realized that if we didn't have this holiday, I would be without the hope and sure knowledge that I will see her again. If God had not become incarnate in the form of Jesus Christ in the first place, salvation would not be a possibility.

That is a great deal about which I should be grateful. And I look at it as the most humbling and breathtaking gift we all were given on that first Christmas, no matter what the date was on which Christ was born.

That is a reason to celebrate.

"A guy can love a million women, but a man can love one woman in a million ways"

GREGG HURWITZ

Christmas Gifts

I opened gifts from Moe this morning, and I consciously chose to face this holiday in a positive, love-affirming way. The gifts that she gave to me were memories that came to my mind as I awoke and prepared for the day. The following are the presents that I received today, wonderful ways that we expressed our love to each other.

How she loved the fact that I would ALWAYS open any and every door for her. At home, getting into the car, at a store or theater, no matter where, I would always open the door. I know that action can be seen by some as sexist in today's world and I want to tell those who perceive it in that manner that it's the way I was raised and I did it to honor the woman I love.

How she would gently poke fun at me when, walking down the street holding hands, I would always switch to the outside, closer to traffic. Moe would say something like, "It's so nice to be walking here in 1880." She knew that it was done that I may be her protector from car splashes, or whatever might come our way.

How Moe would cook a special Christmas dinner for me, every year, which she knew I so thoroughly enjoyed. She would spend hours preparing prime rib (with Kosher salt on the outside and about 10 to fifteen cloves of garlic embedded in it)-the most delicious I ever have eaten. And a blackberry pie, with lattice crust that we joked every year about how it grieved me whenever a guest said yes to a piece that was offered to them as a courtesy.

How we'd, and mostly she'd, spend hours decorating the living room on the night before Christmas so that it would look so special to the kids when they awoke. We'd laugh at the fact that we were the ones who didn't sleep on Christmas Eve.

How she would put up with my foibles-and was always in my corner-no matter what. I am so imperfect. She loved me for who I am, just as I loved her for who she was.

How she was the most unselfish caregiver whenever any of us were sick, even to the detriment of her own health.

How I could always give her a gentle kiss, touch, embrace, and regardless of what she was doing, she would always reciprocate. God, how I miss that.

How she would say, each night as we'd go to bed, "Good night, God bless you, I love you, sweetest dreams of all to you." And I'd follow with, "Good night and I love you." Okay, so I'm not a poet.

How Moe planned four trips as Christmas gifts for me. Three times it was a trip to Washington, D. C., for five days and four nights, with one of our children. We would go on the year they turned ten. She wanted me to show them the city and its historical treasures like I had with her when she was pregnant with our first child, our son.

I had been a tour guide in D. C. in the years before I met Moe, so in a pre-9/11 world, I knew my way around. I hope that the kids cherish those memories as much as I do. Each trip was during February break from school, but the fourth trip was just for me. She sent me to Las Vegas to see my best friend from college, Rich, and she had bought tickets to the Penn and Teller show at the Riviera. Now, I don't gamble, so Las Vegas' charm is lost on me, but Penn and Teller I thoroughly enjoy. Could she have been more unselfish?

I could, and shouldn't, go on and on with the ways we showed our love and devotion to each other, but I will stop to make my point. Christmas can be agonizing for those of us who've lost a loved one. The emptiness-their absence from their rightful place in the day are glaring and the pain can be ever present and wounding. One way to get through it is to remember the gift that they were to our lives. How we, and they, demonstrated it to each other.

Those are Christmas presents that can never get old and by no means ever be taken from us. So, thank you, Moe, for such marvelous presents on this, my first Christmas in 40 years without you.

Merry Christmas, my love.

"Endurance is not just the ability to bear a hard thing, but to turn it into glory"

WILLIAM BARCLAY

The Hits Just Keep On Comin'

I know that I've written about how much I can't wait for this year to be over. The trials and tribulations have seemingly mounted and continued to mount. To add to this state of affairs, I got to spend twelve hours in an emergency ward, out of state, on December 28th. I won't go into all of the lovely details, but I'll just say that the problem was dehydration.

My purpose for this entry is not to complain about the year, or beg for sympathy for my travails. It is to elaborate on how our medical problems can bring back what our loved ones endured prior to their passing.

As I was on my back in the emergency ward room, I vividly remembered those first interminable hours in the hospital when Moe went to the hospital. How the "hurry up and wait" pace seemed unending. How much we appreciated doctors or nurses in the ER who cared, and resented the ones who did not. How, at our age, we wondered if this was the beginning of the end, or something damaging.

But so much more than that, it brought to mind how the end of her life was also the end of suffering. It was the end of waiting, the unknown, guessing, questioning, having to tolerate so much and, simply put, the end.

That brought to mind the old adage that life is not a sprint, it is a marathon. More like a triathlon today. In my case, and perhaps yours, we are no longer participating in a three legged race to the finish, but we are forced to forge onward by ourselves. Not happy about it, for certain. But we also realize that father time is undefeated and there is a finish line somewhere out there.

As we carry on, we can know that our loved ones are resting and free of all of this chaos and concern. In my case, at least, that keeps me moving.

"Do you know that a man is not dead while his name is still spoken?"

TERRY PRATCHETT

The Reaper

As the New Year approached, the typical cartoons appeared online and in newspapers and magazines. 2018 was pictured as a diaper-clad infant, and 2017 was either an old man with a long beard, or someone in a dark hooded robe-like garment.

To me, he should have been equipped with a scythe, and been identified as the grim reaper. The reason I take that position is because I look back on 2017 and see all that was taken from me and my children in that year.

In my case, I lost my love, my partner, my best friend, my confidant, my adviser, my co-conspirator, the rock upon whom my earthly emotional foundation was built, and so much more. Quite a harvest by death, and all it took was brutally snatching the one who was the personification of all those.

Therein lies the secret of victory over 2017. What its passing will not, and cannot possibly do is take memories, impact, legacy, and love with it. Death and separation can do their worst, and boy have they, but she will always be alive in our hearts and in all that she touched.

Her presence there can be terribly painful, and at times it truly is. To focus only on the negative aspects of loss is to give in to the monster and lie emotionally cowering on the ground.

I choose not to submit. With every stroke of angst, I desire to mentally provide a shock and awe level of joyful remembrance. I want to be an oak with roots so deep I cannot be toppled.

After all, Moe and I are still one, forever. So, here we stand.

"My fake plants died because I did not pretend to water them"

MITCH HEDBERG

The Toll

Had to get a haircut yesterday. As I sat in the chair, with nothing to look at in the unforgiving mirror except my head peeking out from the apron, I was reminded of a birthday card I once sent to a cousin of mine. The outside of the card read, *"Time Marches On"*, and the inside had the words, *"Your Face"*. Looking at my reflection I thought that no truer words have ever been conveyed.

Loss and grief take a physical toll on those of us left behind. We can't see it in the immediacy of the moment, but as we trudge on through life without our loved one- with all of that emotional cost we pay, there are bound to be side effects.

We, the grieving, must be conscious of this fact and alert to signs and warnings that our bodies give us about how they are reacting to our emotional state. For some, the effect may be minimal. For others, far too dramatic.

I am reminded of the oft told stories about how when one spouse from a lengthy marriage dies. Within a very short time the other also passes away. I never understood it, but I now get it. They don't necessarily quit living, it is just that the levy on their heart is far too great for them to pay.

The hardest times, for me, are the early morning hours. Coming to consciousness from a long night's sleep, I perceptually live in the netherworld between reality and remembrance. So much is going on in my mind, I often struggle to simply awaken because I either don't want to leave what is happening in my psyche, or I desperately want to get the heck out of there. I know that this is not good for my physical well-being, because I often awaken exhausted. For that reason, I must from now on intentionally focus on my physical condition as I move forward.

They say that the eyes are the window to the soul. If that's the case, mine provide a vista of love, hope, loss and determination to endure. And it ain't a pretty sight.

"Everyone has a plan until they get punched in the mouth"

MIKE TYSON

January 7th

One year ago today, I took Moe to the emergency room. That began a two week siege for her and for her family. I spent every day and night in the hospital, along with my children, as we waged war against her failing heart. Never once in those two weeks did I think that she was not coming home with us. No matter the procedure or "event" as the staff called them. I was always planning on how we would deal with all of this when we took her home.

One of the most quoted, and abused, axioms is that "nobody promised you tomorrow". It seems so trite to me, but it is incredibly true. And the veracity of that became vibrantly evident when she left us.

This is going to be tough to write, and visceral, but it is a lesson that I have learned, and continue to learn to this day. At the very end, I had to say the three hardest words I ever spoke in my life. For reasons that were agonizingly evident and for which I will provide no details here, I looked at the medical staff when it was time and said, "Let her go".

They knew that I was right to do so. I knew that I was doing what Moe would have asked.

I followed those words with the three easiest words I ever spoke, as I held her hand. With all of the strength I could summon, I said "I LOVE YOU!"

There is only one reason I could find the courage to do it. Only one reason I could say those words. I knew for a certainty I was only saying farewell, and not good bye, to her. I knew where she was going and is today, and that is why I could lovingly release her from the suffering.

Someone once said to me, "Want to make God laugh? Tell Him your plans". Well, as far as I am concerned, that is only partially true. Earthly plans? True. Eternal plans? Not true because they are set in stone.

*"If you have God on your side,
everything becomes clear"*

AYRTON SENNA

*January 20*th

So I've reached the appalling anniversary of Moe's death. The vivid memories of those days in the hospital and, far worse still, the moment of her passing have come vibrantly alive in my mind and in my heart.

The entire process of loss and grief have re-emphasized to me how insufficiently equipped we humans are with regard to intimate loss. It has also taught me so many lessons and brought stark realizations to my self-concept. Through this progression of life without my loved one, some of what I have ascertained is encapsulated in the following statements.

I could not have done this…without prayer. Prayer for strength, guidance, forgiveness of sins of omission and commission, for wisdom and discernment, help, loved ones, and for all of the others who grieve. Some prayers are answered in the affirmative with incredibly bright realization, and some are answered with a "No", or "Not now". But, they're answered nevertheless.

I could not have done this…without abandoning control of my life and my grief. It is a requirement, for me. To continually remember that I am NOT in control. I am NOT on the throne. For heaven's sake, last January proved that unequivocally. Instead, I must continue to put all situations, events, and decisions, into the Lord's hands.

I could not have done this…without the support of others. Family, friends, prayerful encouragers, neighbors, and so many others are the ones on whom I consciously and unconsciously lean.

I could not have done this…without determinedly being prepared. We were prepared before Moe went to the hospital and I've addressed this before. I am prepared, for my children's sake, with all of the necessary paperwork should I be called home to be with Him. I must become primed to do whatever is expedient and logically positive with my health, my house, and my other responsibilities.

I could not have done this…without working harder on the tasks of this life. Simply put, half the work force means double the labor. More of what Churchill called "*blood, toil, tears, and sweat*".

I could not have done this…without trying to be a help to others in circumstances like mine. When Theodore Roosevelt's youngest son Quentin's plane was shot down and he was killed at the end of World War I, TR received a letter of condolence from General Pershing. His response is what I would want to repeat to all others who have lost loved ones: "*My dear fellow, you have suffered far more bitter sorrow than has befallen me. You bore it with splendid courage and I should be ashamed of myself if I did not try in a lesser way to emulate that courage.*"

And, most importantly,

I could not have done this…without my Savior. For as long as I can remember, I have believed in Jesus Christ. Early in the year 1958, I publicly accepted Him as my personal Savior and, shortly thereafter, was water baptized. Through all of the years, including the college ones, I never doubted or disbelieved. Did I sin and disobey Him? Abundantly. Was I forgiven when I confessed? Undoubtedly. I have never been one to not declare my belief when asked. I even go to the extreme of giving a short expression of my faith in the Lord when I give a dollar or two to panhandlers.

On January 20th, 2017, at 7:27 PM, in the Cardiac Intensive Care Ward of Beaumont Hospital, my most severe put-up-or-shut-up moment of faith slammed me to the figurative ground. My cherished one and companion of almost 40 years, died while holding my hand. In that maelstrom of anguish, He was there. He comforted me, wept with me, held me, walked with me, guided me, talked to me through His Word, and He has been my encourager ever since.

I really have no idea how those without faith endure this kind of loss. There is only one decision to be made, is this all there is, or is He the Way, the Truth, and the Life? I choose to move forward with, and lean on, Jesus because I can't do it any other way.

"Like all of us in this storm between birth and death, I can wreak no great changes on the world, only small changes for the better, I hope, in the lives of those I love"

DEAN KOONTZ

"If you come to a fork in the road, take it"

YOGI BERRA

And So It Goes

At a particularly tumultuous time in my life at the age of thirty, I hit my knees at the beginning of May in 1977 and told God that I was now ready to settle down if He would show me the woman He had chosen for me. Two weeks later, on a blind date on Friday the 13th, I met her. She was so beautiful, smart, funny, charming, forthright, and all that I could ever have desired. A little over a year later, I married way out of my league when it came to looking at us as a couple. And we stayed married, never doubting our choice and decision.

Now, after a year without her, it is the right time for me to reassess and continue this expedition. At this point, mourning is not a sufficient word for what I'm enduring. The feeling is more like a sense of leaving home without all of the necessary tools and fellow laborer to accomplish the task at hand. She's not coming back and, if she could, she would not put up with any possibility of my becoming stagnant. The hole in me will always be there.

Moe would often jokingly say, "Your next wife won't do this for you" when she would do something special for me. I would always answer with, "Sorry Babe, one life, one wife. Not going to happen." It just isn't possible to love like that more than once.

Well, I still heartily endorse what I said and I also know that I cannot and will not sit here and let the vicissitudes of life come to me. I now consider myself in acquiescence with what is fact. I am in compliance with what this world has forced me to either tolerate or to allow it to emotionally cripple me. I must go out and embrace them, conquer them if I can, endure them if I must, and keep moving forward until I get to whatever God has in store for me. I don't have to like it, but it is reality and reality is that with which we must deal.

The author James Lee Burke wrote, "*I don't believe that acceptance of mortality is a situation you resolve by talking to others. The same for personal grief and mourning or loss of any kind...Sometimes you're the only cat in the cathedral. Ain't nobody else can do it for you.*" I'd add that those truths are only learned through sometimes ominous emotional struggle until the incandescence of their authenticity is apparent.

I once told Moe that, when I went away on trips as a consultant, I was always alone, but never lonely. Now I get to prove that to the extreme.

As she always did, she continues to do. She provides me with inspiration, dedication, and the desire to continue the good work we conceived and conducted together. I will never forget anything about her, and the wound of loss will never fully heal. But that is all part of the journey.

When it comes to my memories of her, I think of the words of the great Welsh poet, Dylan Thomas. I see his sentiments as personifying the conscious act of continuing to remember her and all she was to me. He wrote,

Do not go gentle into that good night,

Old age should burn and rave at the close of day;

Rage, rage, against the dying of the light.

I will not let her memory be air-brushed, or photo shopped, out of my life.

I love you, Moe. Always have, always will.

Meus Bonus Amicus Deus Consultrix

About the Author

Thomas F. Sleete is a born and raised Detroiter. His father was the pastor at Grand River Avenue Baptist Church in Detroit and that is where Tom accepted Christ as his Savior in May of 1958. He was married to his wife, Moe, for 38 ½ hears before her passing and he is the proud father of his son and two daughters, his son-in-law, daughter-in-law, and his granddaughter. A die-hard baseball fan, he lives and dies, figuratively, every summer with his beloved Detroit Tigers. Tom is a teacher with 44 years of classroom experience at Southfield-Lathrup Senior High School in Michigan and Thomas Jefferson High School for Science and Technology in Alexandria, Virginia. He is a historian and some of his favorite individuals in history are Theodore Roosevelt, Winston Churchill, and William F. Buckley, Jr. In addition, he was the Gilder-Lehrman 2005 Michigan History Teacher of the Year. He is currently retired as a classroom teacher but continues to be a consultant for the College Board in AP US History along with several other topics, and resides in Troy, Michigan.